Sugars and Fats

BY BETH BENCE REINKE, MS, RD

The Child's World

Published by The Child's World®
1980 Lookout Drive • Mankato, MN 56003-1705
800-599-READ • www.childsworld.com

Acknowledgments
The Child's World®: Mary Berendes, Publishing Director
Red Line Editorial: Editorial direction
The Design Lab: Design
Amnet: Production
Photographs ©: Front cover: FoodIcons; FoodIcons, 3, 6, 7, 8, 15, 16, 18, 19; Crepesoles/Shutterstock Images, 4; choosemyplate.gov, 5; BrandX Images, 7, 11, 13, 23; PhotoDisc, 8, 9, 10; nito/Shutterstock Images, 12; Stephen VanHorn/Shutterstock Images, 14; Monkey Business Images/Shutterstock Images, 17; skynesher/iStockphoto, 21

ISBN: 978-1623236014
LCCN: 2013931361

Printed in the United States of America
Mankato, MN
July, 2013
PA02178

ABOUT THE AUTHOR

Beth Bence Reinke is a registered dietitian with a master's degree in nutrition from Penn State University. She uses her background in education and pediatric nutrition to help kids learn about healthy eating. Beth is a member of the Academy of Nutrition and Dietetics, a children's author, a magazine writer, and a columnist for her favorite sport, NASCAR.

Table of Contents

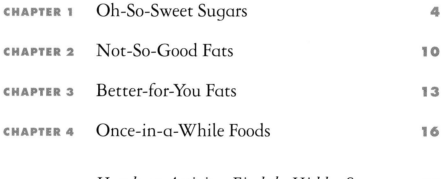

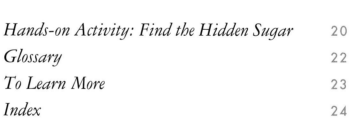

CHAPTER ONE

Oh-So-Sweet Sugars

Sam's class is learning about the MyPlate food guide. MyPlate shows how much to eat from the five food groups: dairy, protein, grains, fruits, and vegetables. The teacher gives each student a food to put in the correct section on the plate. Sam gets a candy bar. Where does it fit on MyPlate?

Sam knows candy is not a dairy food or protein food. A candy bar is not a grain, fruit, or vegetable either. Sam thinks the candy bar does not belong on MyPlate. He is right: There is no space on MyPlate for candy bars. The MyPlate guidelines help kids choose healthy foods. But candy bars and other

▲ Candy bars may taste good, but they don't have a place on MyPlate.

▶ Opposite page: Use the MyPlate diagram to make healthy eating choices.

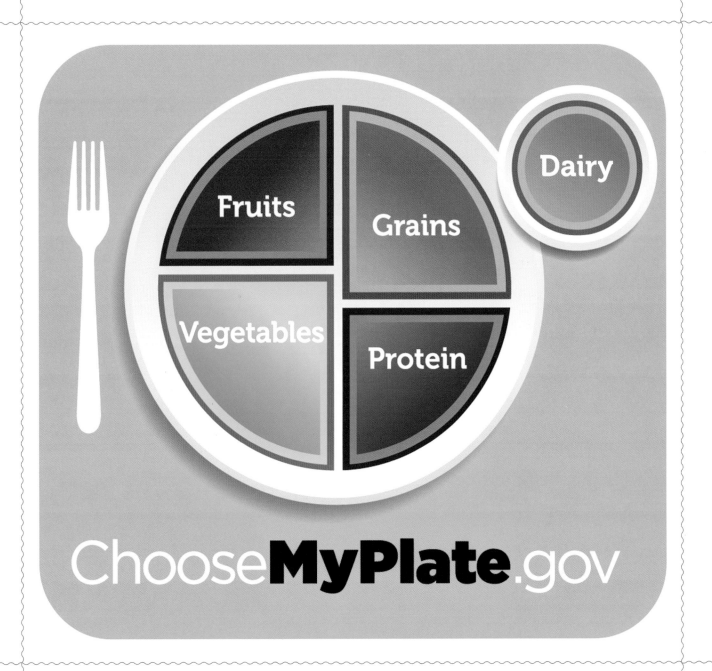

ChooseMyPlate.gov

junk foods are not healthy foods. They contain lots of **added sugars** and fats.

Children in the United States eat or drink about 23 teaspoons of added sugar a day. That is a lot of sugar! Kids get most of it from sweet drinks, desserts, and candy. Too much sugar causes health problems and tooth decay. Learning which foods have sugar helps you make better choices. Eating fewer sweets helps you be healthier.

Did you know there are two kinds of sugars in foods? They are called **natural sugars** and added sugars. Natural sugars are found in foods from nature, such as milk and fruit. Milk sugar is already

▲ Avoid breakfast foods with added sugar, such as doughnuts.

▲ Milk and strawberries are healthy foods with natural sugars.

in milk when it comes from the cow. Fruit sugar is in apples while they are still on the tree. Natural sugars give milk and fruits their delicious flavors. Even though milk and fruits contain natural sugars, they are nutritious foods. Dairy foods and fruits contain many **nutrients** that keep you healthy.

Most of the sugars we eat are the other kind of sugars. Added sugars are not found naturally in foods. They are extra sugars people add to foods. Sugar is added to soda, candy, and ice cream at the factory. Sugar is added to recipes at home, such as muffins or apple pie. What you sprinkle on breakfast cereal at the table is added sugar, too.

Many foods with added sugars are junk foods, such as cookies and doughnuts. But added sugars sneak into other foods, too. Ketchup tastes sweet because it has sugar. Added sugar hides in salad dressing and spaghetti sauce.

Sugar has many different names. All of these words mean sugar: cane juice, corn sweetener, corn syrup, fruit juice concentrate, high-fructose corn syrup, honey, malt syrup, molasses, and nectar. Words that end with "-ose" are sugars, too:

- dextrose
- fructose
- glucose
- lactose
- maltose
- sucrose

▲ **An ice cream sundae has added sugar in its ice cream, syrup, and whipped cream.**

SUGAR, SUGAR, WHERE ARE YOU HIDING?

Wondering where added sugar is hiding in your food? All these popular foods have at least a teaspoon of added sugar:

French salad dressing
   (2 tablespoons) = 1 teaspoon
fruit punch (1 cup) =
   7 teaspoons
graham cracker (1 large
   rectangle) = 1 teaspoon
ketchup (1 tablespoon) =
   1 teaspoon
soda (12-ounce can) =
   10 teaspoons
spaghetti sauce (1/2 cup) =
   2 teaspoons

▶ Chocolate chip cookies are sweet treats that have added sugar.

To find sneaky sugars, check the ingredients list on the package. If you spot any of these words, the food has added sugar.

CHAPTER TWO

Not-So-Good Fats

Fats give you energy. They also help your body grow and develop properly. MyPlate does not have a section on the plate for fats. But everybody needs to eat some fats to stay healthy. Some fats are better for you. Other kinds are not so good.

Solid fats are not-so-good fats. The fats are called solid because they stay firm at room temperature. Eating too much solid fat is bad for the heart. MyPlate reminds us to eat less solid fat. One easy way is to drink lower-fat milk. Another way is to eat lean meats such as

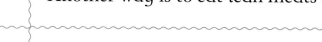

▼ Replace fatty foods such as hot dogs with chicken or turkey breasts.

► Potato chips have a lot of trans fats and are not a healthy snack.

TRANS FATS ARE TRICKY! Sometimes a label shows "zero grams trans fat" when there is trans fat in a food. If there is only a small amount of trans fat per serving, the label is allowed to say zero. Isn't that tricky? When it says zero grams trans fat, the only way to be sure is to check the ingredients list. If you see the word "**hydrogenated**" on the ingredients list, that food does have trans fat. Always look in both places to be sure.

turkey and chicken instead of sausage, hot dogs, and bacon.

There are two kinds of solid fats: **saturated fats** and **trans fats**. Saturated fats come from animal foods. They are found in meats, milk, cheese, and butter. Sausage, bacon, and hot dogs have a lot of saturated fats.

Trans fats are solid fats, too. Trans fats are created by changing liquid oils to make them solid. The trans fats help foods stay fresh longer on the store shelf. But trans fats are not good for your health. In fact, it is best to eat no trans fats at all. Trans fats hide in many snack foods and baked goods. Some kinds of crackers, cookies, and doughnuts have trans fats. Other foods may have trans fats, too: frozen pizza, margarine, frosting in a tub, biscuits, and french fries, just to name a few.

Reading food labels can help you eat less solid fat. A food's Nutrition Facts Label shows how much fat is in a serving. Remember, saturated fats and trans fats are not-so-good fats. Choose foods with the lowest amounts of these fats.

▲ A pile of french fries contains a lot of not-so-good fats.

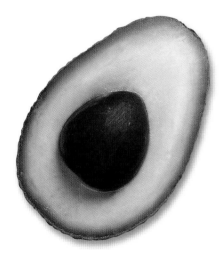

▲ Avocados are a great source of healthy fats.

CHAPTER THREE

Better-for-You Fats

Oils are better-for-you fats. They are found in seafood, nuts, avocadoes, and olives. Some oils come from plants such as peanuts, sunflowers, and corn. Healthy oils are liquid at room temperature. That is why they can be poured from a bottle. Healthy oils taste great with vegetables. Broccoli and carrots are delicious stir-fried in peanut oil. Olive oil mixed with vinegar and herbs makes a zesty salad dressing.

Remember, oils do not have a space on MyPlate. That is because most people do not eat plain fats. You would not slurp a teaspoon of olive oil, right? Instead, fats are added to foods in cooking or as a sauce. Some fats are already inside the food, such as oils in seafood and nuts.

Most of the fats in oils are called **unsaturated fats**. On the Nutrition Facts Label, there are two kinds. They seem like big words. But both have "unsaturated" at the end and smaller words in

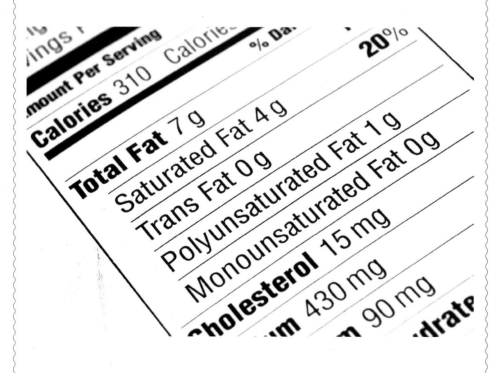

FATS ON THE LABEL
Look at this Nutrition Facts Label. The solid fats and healthy oils are shown for you.

Solid fats = not-so-good fats = saturated fat and trans fat
Healthy oils = better-for-you fats = polyunsaturated fat and monounsaturated fat

You can read Nutrition Facts Labels to see how much of each kind of fat is in a food. Try to choose foods with less solid fat and no trans fat. Eat foods with healthy oils instead of solid fats.

◄ Look for monounsaturated and polyunsaturated fats on a food's nutrition label.

front. The two kinds are polyunsaturated fat and monounsaturated fat. Look on the Nutrition Facts Label to find these healthy oils. MyPlate reminds us to eat healthy oils instead of solid fats. Here are some ideas:

- Eat a tuna fish sandwich instead of a hot dog.
- Ask an adult to cook sliced potatoes in oil instead of butter.
- Eat a handful of nuts instead of snack crackers.
- Have a turkey sandwich instead of grilled cheese.

▶ **Nuts make a great anytime snack.**

CHAPTER FOUR

Once-in-a-While Foods

▼ Candies such as jelly beans are okay to eat every once in a while.

Foods with lots of sugars or fats are junk foods. Think of junk foods as once-in-a-while foods. Eating a cupcake at a birthday party is a special treat. But it is not good to gobble up junk foods every day.

Television ads try to make kids believe junk foods are yummy. Commercials show kids having fun while eating junk foods or fast foods. The sugary, fatty snacks come in colorful boxes. But do not let nice boxes or

▶ Trade fatty junk foods for healthy meals.

FAST FOOD? YOU CAN CUT THE FAT AND SUGAR!
Fast foods are once-in-a-while treats. They have lots of solid fats and sugars. But you can choose healthier fast foods. Next time you eat fast food:

- Choose a grilled chicken sandwich more often than a burger, fried chicken, or chicken nuggets.
- Ask for no cheese when you have a burger.
- Ask for a side order of fruit more often than french fries.
- Drink non-fat milk or water instead of a milkshake or soda.

commercials trick you. Foods full of sugars and fats are not healthy.

Junk is trash. It is not good stuff. Junk foods are not good stuff either. They are full of sugar and fat. Junk foods have few nutrients such as **vitamins** and **minerals**. Most junk foods do not have fiber either. People in the United States eat too much junk food. They eat almost three times as many added sugars and solid fats as they should.

17

MyPlate reminds us to eat less sugar and replace solid fats with healthy oils. That is easy, right? Just eat fewer junk foods and more healthy foods. Healthy foods taste yummy. They have lots of nutrients for your body.

To find healthier foods, remember to look on the Nutrition Facts Label and ingredients lists. Choose foods that are lower in sugars and solid fats.

▲ Popcorn is a yummy whole-grain snack.

Instead of	Choose
snack crackers	whole-wheat pretzels
a candy bar	graham crackers dipped in yogurt
a cupcake	a homemade fruit muffin
tortilla chips	popcorn
candies	nuts
ice cream	low-fat frozen yogurt
beef jerky stick	banana
potato chips and dip	raw veggies and dip

Fill up the MyPlate way! Put fruits and vegetables on half of your plate. Place protein and grain foods on the other side. Have a glass of low-fat milk to drink. MyPlate has no spot for junk foods. Save junk foods for once-in-a-while treats. Eat tasty foods from the MyPlate food groups every day.

▶ Stir-fry is a delicious and healthy meal.

Hands-on Activity: Find the Hidden Sugar

Added sugar is sneaky. It hides in lots of foods. Is there hidden sugar in your breakfast cereal? You can find out.

What You'll Need:

breakfast cereal boxes in your kitchen or at your grocery store

Directions:

1. First, look in the cupboards for breakfast cereals. Or look at cereals at the grocery store. Then, sit the boxes side-by-side so you can see the nutrition facts labels. Which cereal has the most sugar per serving? Which one has the least amount of sugar?

2. Look on the ingredients list for each cereal. Find all the ingredients that are added sugar. For a reminder of words that mean sugar, go back to chapter one.

Glossary

added sugars (AD-ed SHUG-erz): Added sugars are sugars that are added to foods at the factory, during cooking, or at the table. Candy and soda have added sugars.

hydrogenated (hi-DRAH-jen-ayt-id): Hydrogenated describes a healthy oil that was made into a solid fat. Trans fats are hydrogenated.

junk foods (JUNK foodz): Junk foods are foods that are high in fat or sugar, such as cakes and doughnuts. Junk foods contain added sugars and fats, but few nutrients.

minerals (MIN-er-ulz): Minerals are substances found in foods. Minerals help the body stay healthy.

natural sugars (NACH-ur-ul SHUG-erz): Natural sugars are sugars found in foods naturally. Fruits and milk contain natural sugars.

nutrients (NOO-tree-ents): Nutrients are substances the body needs to grow. Vitamins and minerals are nutrients.

oils (OY-ulz): Oils are fats that are liquid at room temperature. Oils in our foods can come from plants and seafood.

saturated fats (SACH-ur-ayt-id fats): Saturated fats are solid fats found mostly in animal foods. Meats and dairy contain saturated fats.

solid fats (SOL-id fats): Solid fats are fats that are solid at room temperature. Solid fats include trans fats and saturated fats.

trans fats (trans fats): Trans fats are solid fats created from vegetable oils. Small amounts of trans fats do not need to be included on a Nutrition Facts Label.

unsaturated fats (un-SACH-ur-ayt-id fats): Unsaturated fats are fats found mostly in liquid oils from vegetables, fish, and nuts. Unsaturated fats include polyunsaturated fats and monounsaturated fats.

vitamins (VYE-tuh-minz): Vitamins are substances found in foods that help the body stay healthy. Vitamins are found in fruits and vegetables.

To Learn More

BOOKS

Goodrow, Carol. *Happy Feet, Healthy Food: Your Child's First Journal of Exercise and Healthy Eating.* Halcottsville, NY: Breakaway Books, 2004.

Zinczenko, David. *Eat This, Not That! For Kids!: Be the Leanest, Fittest Family on the Block!* Emmaus, PA: Rodale, 2008.

WEB SITES

Visit our Web site for links about sugars and fats: **childsworld.com/links**

Note to Parents, Teachers, and Librarians: We routinely verify our Web links to make sure they are safe and active sites. So encourage your readers to check them out!

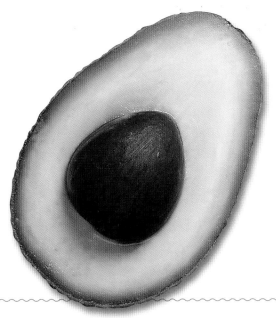

Index